CHICKENS

ARE...

(*personally hand-drawn by aurelia nobleia)

for Edward and Laura Yong

turnip.co

CHICKENS
ARE...

49 ways chickens inspire, entertain,
and make you happier everyday

Aurelia Nobleia

... like potato chips,
you can't
have just one

I'll raise just one

One year later...

eggs-amples of eggs-ellence

the best at
getting their hair done

the most huggable things ever

repeat offenders

trusty head-warmers

cool with glasses

'Sorry, I can't... I have to walk my chicken!'

great excuses to get away

your holiday decor's
worst nightmare

secretly experts in the art of cuteness

solar-powered alarm clocks

your best feather babies

the ultimate cockstars

broody

free-range, free-riders

automated lawn mowers
and pest controllers

the undisputed fashionistas
of the barnyard

stand-up comedi-hens

honest fowl players

poultry in motion

cluck-wise

swimmers

incredible at egg-onomics

just so hen-tertaining

free loaders

eggs-purts at
stealing yer food

better gifts than roses

oh no... not this

THE EGGO NEWS
FOWL DECEPTION
Chicken Pretends to Be Sick To Get Free Mealworms At Vet
WING CLIPPING 101

very cocky about
their image

always searching for adventure
(and mealworms)

intimidating with 3d-printed arms

ardent peck-abooers

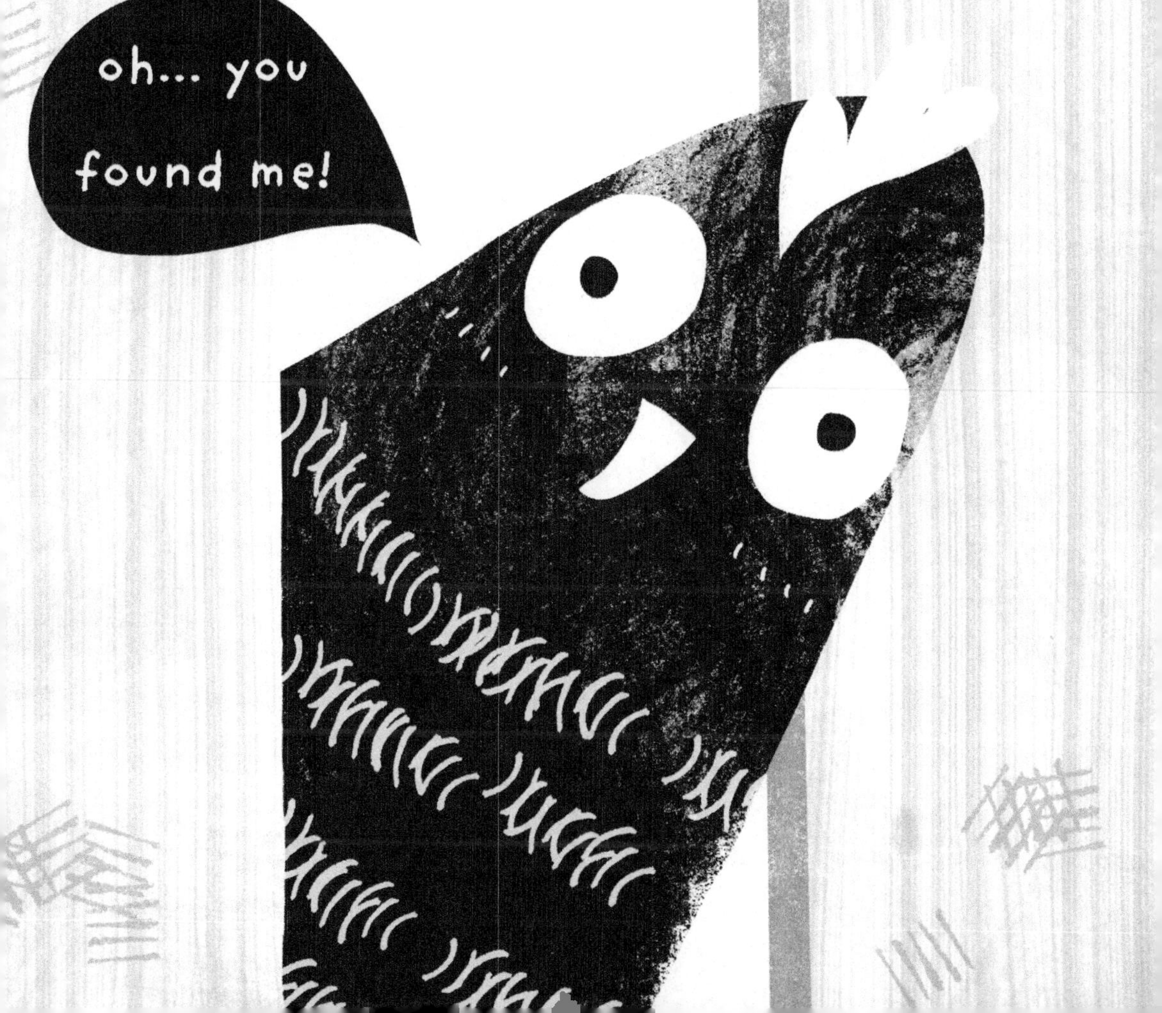

lacy footprint
artists in winter

better intelligence agents
than pigeons

great leaders!
...they don't tell
you what to do...
they show you
how it's done

your faithful security guards

heart-warming mothers

cups of cuteness

better bath companions
than rubber ducks

fluffy butts with a charm

peck-nic party legends

egg-squisite scholars

a bookworm's
greatest enemies

a baker's biggest fan

rulers of the roost

never resistant to the grooming
services of a hoo-man servant

FARM FRESH

the reason to have a fancy
egg sorter in your kitchen,
so you always remember
to eat the oldest egg first

thinking buddies with you
when you're pondering the
labyrinth of life's perplexities

always staring at you with a face
so serious, you'd think you just got
in trouble with your ma and pa

always craving egg-stra
attention and praise

Pssstt.... hey... feathered friends!

If my book has brightened your coop or made your day more hen-tertaining, could you help spread the feathers and leave a review?

Your words not only support the author's hard work but also boost the book's visibility, putting the spotlight on chicken chuckles and hen happiness. So someone else can get a laugh. And brighten their day.

It's free. And takes less than 60 seconds.

It's a clucky crusade! Your reviews are golden eggs, helping our cause and building a better world with chickens.

Plus, a little birdie (that's me!) will be personally reading all the reviews, and feeding on them as fuel for their next work. So, let's unite our clucks and create a global parade of positivity. Your winged words make a difference!

Thank you from the bottom of my heart. Now, let's go out and get some more chickens!

Printed in Great Britain
by Amazon